Original title:
Inside the Front Door

Copyright © 2025 Creative Arts Management OÜ
All rights reserved.

Author: Victor Mercer
ISBN HARDBACK: 978-1-80587-136-1
ISBN PAPERBACK: 978-1-80587-606-9

A World Woven of Thresholds

A carpet of socks strewn near the shoes,
Dancing with dust bunnies, they like to amuse.
Welcome mat grinning, it's quite the old charmer,
Greeted by laughter, no hint of the drama.

The coat rack's a circus, each jacket a clown,
Hats piled so high, they might tumble down.
Keys jingle like maracas, a tune they all know,
As they wait for the day's exciting new show.

The mirror reflects chaos, a whimsically scene,
Where socks may be missing, but smiles intervene.
Whispers of secrets from corners so small,
Echoing giggles that bounce off the walls.

With every new arrival, the jests intertwine,
Creating a quilt of good times and good wine.
Laughter erupts as the door creaks wide,
In this lively realm where joys coincide.

The First Step In

A squeaky floor begins to croak,
Like a grumpy old man who just woke.
Shoes scattered like leaves in the fall,
Always find the cat's paw on the wall.

Hats stacked high in a silly pile,
Each one whispers a quirky style.
Baskets of keys dance a jig,
Woe to those who pick the wrong twig.

Secrets of the Entryway

A coat rack grins with tangled pride,
It's a jungle where jackets collide.
Umbrellas corpses from storms before,
Waiting for sun, but still wanting more.

A mirror reflects a quirky cheer,
As if it's laughing, bright and clear.
Each visit to this odd little nook,
Brings secrets and smiles, just take a look.

Greeted by Shadows

Shadows dance as if on cue,
The old lamp flickers, adding to the brew.
A friendly ghost might just pop by,
As I trip over shoes stacked awry.

The mat says 'Welcome,' but whispers 'Run!'
To surprise me as I seek some fun.
Laughter echoes in this cozy space,
Where every corner hides a face.

Hushed Moments of Arrival

A pause at the threshold, breath held tight,
The clock ticks loudly in the starlit night.
The door creaks open with a gentle moan,
As I step boldly into the unknown.

A pile of mail spills secrets untold,
Some bills, a postcard, a flyer so bold.
The welcome mat's witty with words so sweet,
But it quakes underneath my dancing feet.

Entryway Echoes

The shoes pile high, it's quite the sight,
A solo sock joins in the fight.
Do we ever know, just what we own?
The echoes of chaos, a funny tone.

A coat rack stands, arms flailing wide,
Hats and scarves in a lively ride.
Each time we enter, it dances with glee,
Calling for help - or maybe just tea!

Secrets of the Foyer

What lurks in the shadows, we cannot know,
A dust bunny kingdom, with no way to go.
The lamp's flickering, like a shy little star,
Whispering secrets, not going too far.

Beneath the mat, a treasure awaits,
An old key, perhaps, to someone's great fate.
Or maybe just crumbs from last night's feast,
An entryway legend, from the east!

The Space Between Welcome

Here lies the space, neither here nor there,
Where coats get lost but we don't really care.
A pile of bags, a misfit design,
The crammed little corner, oh so divine.

As friends arrive, they giggle and sigh,
"Is it a home or a clothing supply?"
We laugh it off, it's just our style,
A welcoming mess, bringing joy all the while!

Threshold of Dreams

Step right up to a hallway of cheer,
Where dreams are whispered, and laughter draws near.
Forgotten umbrellas begin to take flight,
Parade of the absurd, what a lovely sight!

A welcome mat grins, "Please leave your woe,"
As we gather our stories, our fun little show.
With every footstep, the mysteries bloom,
In a world where silliness finds ample room!

The Frame of Familiarity

The welcome mat greets all with a grin,
Socks that don't match, oh where to begin?
Couches that double as treasure chests,
And snacks that attract all kinds of quests.

Jackets tossed like confetti on floors,
Where laughter spills out from unseen doors.
A dance party starts with each quirky thud,
As dust bunnies roll in a land of pure fun.

Pictures askew, framed with pure charm,
Each face tells a tale, with endless warmth.
A space where the chaos feels right at home,
And everyone knows not to zone out and roam.

Full of quirks, like a sitcom scene,
Where life is absurd and bright, not mean.
You step through the frame, leave worries behind,
And find that each moment's a treasure to find.

Where Heartbeats Pause

A rubber plant waves with a leafy cheer,
Ticking clocks laugh as they shed a tear.
Old carpets tell stories through every stain,
They might just be magic, with a hint of pain.

The fridge hums a tune, both old and new,
It guards pickles' secrets, like a jealous boo.
Inside lies a treasure, a slice of unbaked pie,
That whispers, 'Don't leave me, oh, please do not try!'

Post-its are scattered, like birds on a wire,
Each note a reminder of what we require.
From laundry to laughter, it all gets stored,
In moments we cherish, in life we adored.

Here, time takes a breather, a comical show,
Where heartbeats can giggle and bounce to and fro.
Each pause a punchline, each silence a jest,
It's the place where the joy is simply the best.

Behind the Knotted Key

The old key hangs on a hook with pride,
Looks like a prop from a magician's ride.
It twists and it turns, a puzzle to see,
Unlocking the stories that dance with glee.

Past echoes and laughter spin tales in the air,
Like socks in a dryer, they swirl without care.
Each door that you open, a whiff of surprise,
Like finding a squirrel in a hat of disguise!

The cupboard's a concert with spices that sing,
While the chairs have debates on who's reigning king.
A sausage dog snoozes, a king on his throne,
With dreams of the pizza that's ordered at dawn.

So twist that old key and let laughter unfold,
These moments, my friend, are worth more than gold.
For behind every knot, there's a treasure untold,
A life that's amusing, a joy to behold.

Chamber of First Impressions

A door creaks open with a curious squeak,
Where the breath of fresh cookies is quite the tweak.
The air hums a tune, as chairs jiggle near,
A room full of warmth, and heartfelt cheer.

The floorboards rejoice in a welcoming dance,
While raccoons in slippers plot their own chance.
First impressions glitter like confetti at play,
Where charm meets chaos in a jumbled ballet.

The walls bear witness to laughter and dreams,
As echoes bounce back like chiming of streams.
Each smile a passport, each giggle a key,
Unfolding the magic of you and of me.

In this merry chamber, we sip on delight,
Trading tales under twinkling fairy light.
With every new visitor, a story ignites,
In the heart of a home, where everything's bright.

An Invitation to Rest

Come sit upon this cozy chair,
With cushions soft, it's a delight.
The cat may steal your place, beware,
But snoring humans will feel right.

Take off your shoes, let laughter ring,
The socks you wear might start a show.
We'll sip some tea and dance, I sing,
And awkward moves will steal the show.

The kettle's whistling, oh what fun,
Bring out the snacks, don't be too shy.
The party's waiting, let's all run,
As long as we don't trip and fly!

So grab a plate, don't hold back now,
Beneath this roof, we'll have a blast.
With joy and jests, we'll take a bow,
A memory made, forever cast!

Guardian of the Entryway

I stand here tall, so proud and bright,
To greet you with a quirky smile.
My squeaky hinges bring delight,
And make you pause, just for a while.

Oh, silly shoes, they trip and fall,
In my threshold, they all collide.
A dance of laughter, one and all,
As they shed dirt and joy, they slide.

I'm but a frame, a wooden gate,
To family, friends, anyone, come near.
You'll find me always, never late,
With shades of warmth and playful cheer.

Inside I spy, on all the fun,
With memories clanking like old pots.
So swing me wide, let games be spun,
For I'm the guardian of your plots!

Navigating the Threshold

Step right up, don't be so shy,
This is where we laugh and play.
Just mind your head as you pass by,
 Or bumping in will ruin the day!

Bring your quirkiest tales to share,
I promise hearts will crack a grin.
With sticky floors and cat hair,
 It's chaos where the fun begins!

Face the wall, or the sock brigade,
Which laundry won't get lost today?
With clinking cups, the mess parade,
We'll weave our night, come what may.

So grab a friend, form a long line,
We'll navigate this playful place.
Together we'll be, just feel fine,
In this wild space, we'll find our grace!

The Quiet Unfolding

Come gather round, the day unwinds,
Where laughter floats like gentle air.
Amid the clutter, joy reminds,
With tales that bubble everywhere.

We'll share a look, a wink, a grin,
As slippers dance across the floor.
It's in the chaos we begin,
To craft the tales we all adore.

The pantry waits with snacks galore,
Be careful now, those cookies tease.
With every bite, we laugh and roar,
Carefree moments that aim to please.

So here we sit, with hearts so full,
A refuge built on joy and jest.
In cozy corners, thoughts will pull,
This quiet space is simply the best!

Passages of the Heart

A hallway beckons with squeaky floors,
Where socks and shoes, like best friends, soar.
The cat surveys her royal domain,
While dust bunnies plot a silly campaign.

A mirror grins with a quirky face,
Reflecting battles in this wacky space.
A knock at the wall, a ghost may tease,
Or is that just Uncle Fred sneezing with ease?

The fridge hums tales of leftovers grand,
With pickles dancing, a jar of jam planned.
The couch holds secrets, a popcorn stash,
Each crumb a memory, a hidden trash.

Yet laughter bubbles through each whacky route,
With every step, a chuckle or two about.
A home of quirks, nonsense fills the air,
Where joy skips and bounces without a care.

Between the Frames

Pictures hang with cheeky grins,
Captured moments, wild spins.
A dog in a tutu, a cat with flair,
Frame by frame, we giggle and stare.

The clock ticks funny, always late,
For tea parties with the neighbor's mate.
Each tick a reminder of playful glee,
As time dances silly, quite merrily.

Beneath the frames, the chaos lies,
Board games scattered, a mischievous surprise.
Marbles roll like they're in a race,
While grandma's knitting turns into lace.

A scene unfolds, and we all collide,
From laughter to puzzlement, no need to hide.
Between the frames, life's amusing dance,
Each snapshot a tale, a whimsical chance.

Where Echoes Reside

Whispers bounce off the walls with cheer,
Chasing echoes that hold us near.
The dog chases shadows, a sight to behold,
While mugs of coffee spill laughter untold.

Footsteps stomp with exaggerated grace,
As the kids declare a pillow fight space.
The echo of giggles fills every room,
A symphony born from innocent whim.

Napping in corners, the cat takes charge,
Plotting his dreams, oh, so large!
While socks play hide-and-seek, on the run,
Tickling toes until laughter's begun.

Here in this haven, where echoes convene,
Life's a parade of the silly and keen.
With each silly sound, and every embrace,
We craft our own joy, our peculiar space.

Unveiling Familiarity

Beneath the rug, socks make a home,
A mischievous place, no need to roam.
Here's the laundry monster, looming so large,
Decorated in colors, odd and at large.

The fridge door creaks, a comedic scene,
As leftovers plot, wait, what does this mean?
The ice cream's winking, the veggies all pout,
In this funny circus, there's no doubt.

The chair squeaks loud, with every twist,
A musical seat, can it be missed?
Slippers join forces in a cozy dance,
Welcoming toes to their warm, fluffy chance.

Unveiling moments where laughter resides,
In every nook, where fun abides.
This sanctuary whispers its gentle tune,
As the sun peeks in, we giggle at noon.

Latch and Lullaby

A creak and a groan, what a silly refrain,
As shoes scatter wildly in a comical chain.
The dog steals a sock, oh what a delight,
While cats play the drums on the kitchen light.

The visitor's face, a portrait of shock,
Stepping on squishies and old rubber cock.
With laughter we enter, a circus of fun,
Where furniture's laughing, and chores never done.

Kids tumble like marbles, all giggles and glee,
They build a tall fortress, just wait and see!
Hiding in corners, they peek out to play,
A launchpad for mischief, a whimsical stay.

So welcome, dear friend, to this jumble of cheer,
Where laughter's the music, and joy is near.
With every small step, prepare for a show,
A laugh or a slip—oh, you never will know!

Tapestry of Footfalls

Step right in, if you dare,
But watch for the cat now, don't give him a scare.
He's weaving through shoes like a thread through a lace,
While dad trips on carpets with the most awkward grace.

The floorboards are squeaky, a symphony sweet,
As children concoct their most clumsy retreat.
A tumble, a giggle, a dance in the hall,
In this tapestry woven, we all have a ball.

Come savor the moments of mildly absurd,
As snacks fly like missiles, excitingly blurred.
Each footfall a story, each laugh a new thread,
As socks become superheroes, ahead of the spread!

Here's to the chaos, the smiles, oh my!
With friends by the door, and laughter held high.
In this patchwork of bliss, we stumble and blend,
Life's funniest moments, where humor won't end!

The Glistening Threshold

Oh what a scene at this sparkling gate,
Where muddy shoes gather, but who can relate?
The mat winks at you, almost wearing a grin,
As giggles and snacks get a new kind of spin.

The doorbell chimed in a silly old way,
A chorus of rumbles, it's livening day.
With every new visitor barging right through,
It feels like a circus, a funny hullabaloo.

Jackets flop on the couch like lazy old cats,
As kids throw confetti, or maybe just hats.
Each face tells a story of laughter and play,
Erupting like popcorn, all night and all day.

So slide on your socks, come dance in the sun!
In the most awkward shuffle, our hearts beat as one.
This threshold's a treasure, where giggles abound,
In the spark of each moment, true joy can be found!

First Breath of Solitude

Ah, quiet now falls with each gentle creak,
A moment of peace, oh, isn't it meek?
But who sneezed so loud? It broke all the calm,
A symphony started, a rather odd psalm.

The couch has a tale, it whispers of snacks,
Of crumbs that escaped all our diligent hacks.
The plants start to smile with each passing breeze,
As dust bunnies play tag between the chairs and the trees.

A cat pounces forth, a knight on his quest,
To conquer the sunbeams and claim the best rest.
But just as he stretches, a loud dizzy whir,
The vacuum takes notice; oh what a stir!

So solitude's sighs become laughter-filled calls,
As the world comes alive with its bumps and its brawls.
For in moments so still, the humor runs rife,
With quirks and with chuckles, we savor this life!

Whispers from the First Step

The mat says 'Welcome', but I just sigh,
It's a portal for shoes, oh my, oh my!
A welcome of chaos, no grandeur to flaunt,
Mismatched socks and a pet that won't jaunt.

Beneath the coat rack, a jungle of fluff,
Whiskers and tangles, it's all just too rough.
The shoes are a puzzle, a game of hide and seek,
Wondering who wore what, so unique, so chic.

A door that swings wide with stories untold,
Adventures in slippers, both timid and bold.
Tiptoe through laughter, a dance on the floor,
Each step is a giggle, who could ask for more?

Here lies the welcome, a playful embrace,
With a grin and a wink, it's a nutty place.
So kick off your shoes, join the cacophony,
In this mad little home, you'll find harmony.

The Veil of Everyday

The door swings wide, what a curious sight,
Laundry on chairs, oh what a delight!
The fridge hums a tune, a serenade sweet,
Yet it's bursting with leftovers no one can eat.

Shadows of slippers line up in a row,
Waiting for feet that have nowhere to go.
A cat on the windowsill judging the scene,
While I fluff up the couch like it's fit for a queen.

Dishes pile high, like a mountain of dreams,
Each plate tells a story, or so it seems.
Not a single incident goes without flair,
With socks in the toaster and crumbs in the chair.

The daily parade of the absurd unfolds,
Where laughter is cheap, and the silliness holds.
So grab a good book, let the chaos reign,
In this veil of routine, there's fun to gain.

The Journey Starts Here

With a jingle of keys, off we go bold,
A quest to the couch, where the remote is gold.
The snacks are now packed, the cat's in the way,
The journey of comfort won't let us stray.

Through the wild terrain of unkempt hair,
We dodge all the socks, hoping not to stare.
The fridge is a treasure chest full of treats,
Yet I'm stuck on the couch – guess I can't eat!

Adventure through podcasts, the laughter's on high,
Perfecting the art of the sit and the sigh.
With pillows as shields, we laugh as we brawl,
For the journey to chill is the greatest of all.

So pack up your worries, your fears take a nap,
For this odyssey's charm is sweet as a wrap.
Hold on to the remote; let the marathon start,
The journey of leisure is a work of art.

Fragments of Affection

Each thing has a story, a history strange,
A sippy cup left, how could it rearrange?
A love note to chocolate, "I miss you, my dear,"
Who knew such sweet sentiments lingered near?

The wall hosts a collage of scribbles and glee,
Crayon masterpieces, the joy of the spree.
Toys crowd the hall as if caught in a dance,
Each fragment of laughter just waiting its chance.

Leftover birthday cake, a sugary fest,
Each bite a reminder that we are all blessed.
The fridge whispers secrets of dinners long gone,
As we treasure these moments, we cling to the fun.

In a place where the chaos meets heartfelt delight,
Every oddity shines in the warm evening light.
Fragments of love make a tapestry bright,
In this cozy little chaos, all feels just right.

Markers of Passage

A stack of shoes, all out of line,
A dog runs through with socks to dine.
Crumbs and chaos, a daily race,
Who knew home could be such a space?

There's a coat rack wearing hats like crowns,
And an umbrella with a mind that frowns.
Each corner seems to whisper loud,
"Are we a family or just a crowd?"

Footprints lead like a treasure map,
Where did the cat go? Oh, what a trap!
Sudden laundry takes the stage,
Furballs rolling, a comical rage.

But still we laugh as we clean the mess,
Each new adventure is just the best.
This wacky place, our own abode,
Laugh lines deepened along the road.

Entryways to Remember

The door swings open with a creak,
Welcoming gales of chatter and cheek.
A shoehorn battles against the pile,
And a doormat grins with a cheeky smile.

The keys jingle like a merry band,
As the pizza guy nervously stands.
"Is that a cat? Oh, what a sight!"
He dashes off—no tip in sight.

Pictures hang askew on the wall,
Spilling over stories, big and small.
Entryway jokes often take flight,
Who thought that hall could be so bright?

Beneath the coats, a child hides low,
Poking her head out for the show.
Yet every moment here we hold,
Turns to a tale we'll forever be told.

Threshold Whispers

Laughter spills from an open space,
As guests amble in, finding their place.
The doorbell rings like a jester's call,
Who knew a threshold could be so tall?

A vacuum sleeps in the corner's den,
Whispering gossip of dust bunnies' kin.
"Is that chocolate? No, just the cat,"
Who knew a home could be such a spat?

Jackets hang like they're having a ball,
How many times will we trip and fall?
Each evening here draws friends so near,
Every silly story sparks a cheer.

As we wander through, maps in our mind,
The best of times are the ones unrefined.
For every hiccup and every flare,
Is a moment cherished, without a care.

Beyond the Welcome Mat

A squeaky floor with a heart that sings,
Regales of comedies and oddball things.
Beneath the mat lies tales galore,
Who forgot the keys once more?

Footprints splashed with muddy cheer,
Socks that refuse to reappear.
Laughter bubbles as friends collide,
In this land of embrace, we abide.

A random hat on the kitchen chair,
Confetti left from a past affair.
This messy haven, our favorite dive,
Where every blunder keeps us alive.

Each new face wears an eager grin,
As we navigate the thick and thin.
This cozy chaos is where we find,
Joyful moments all intertwined.

Threshold Whispers

At the edge where shoes collide,
Mismatched socks and cats abide.
The welcome grin of a dusty chair,
Awaits the tales we choose to share.

In every creak of wood and floor,
There's a secret that begs for more.
A jester's hat hangs from the hook,
Whispers giggle like a good book.

As keys jingle like a tune so sweet,
Adventures linger, ready to greet.
With every blink, the world stands still,
What's next to come? A wild thrill!

So drop your bags, release that sigh,
In this nook, the heart can fly.
Thresholds may shift, but joy is found,
In the laughter that knows no bound.

Unseen Sanctuary

A fortress made of fallen leaves,
Where quiet chuckles dance and weave.
Sock puppets hide in the cupboard's depth,
Hosting parties with laughter kept.

Underneath the dust and grime,
Lies a treasure of silly rhyme.
A fridge that hums a tune so bright,
Offers leftovers ready for a bite.

In the corners where shadows linger,
Ghostly giggles raise a finger.
Stand a moment, feel the air,
It tickles lightly, but do not scare!

An unseen world, a playful jest,
Where every object wears a vest.
Knock, knock jokes ring through the hall,
In this realm, we're all quite small.

Beneath the Welcome Mat

A secret place where crumbs reside,
Beneath the mat that's worn with pride.
Old jokes and stories keep it neat,
Awaiting shoes with friendly feet.

Dust bunnies waltz in cha-cha sways,
While time drips slowly through fun-filled days.
Every flap of the door reveals,
Joyful laughter that time conceals.

Puddles of sunshine greet the gloom,
As boots kick all the dirt and doom.
Life spins in a carousel of cheer,
A wacky world, come quickly near!

With a stomp and clap, we call it home,
Through silly antics, we freely roam.
Dropping off doubts, we take a chance,
Under this mat, let joy enhance!

Echoes of Home

In the hallway where echoes linger,
Playful voices dance like a singer.
Every step upon the stair,
Resonates with giggles and air.

Bouncing lights from ceiling beams,
Chase away those sleepy dreams.
The clock ticks on, a funny tune,
As shadows sway like a cartoon.

Whiskers twitch from the shelf's high place,
Squirrels chitter with a silly grace.
From every corner, the laughter spreads,
Tales aplenty, like yarns in threads.

So gather 'round and let it beam,
This echo chamber of our dream.
With hearts wide open, let's take a peek,
For in each laugh, the magic speaks.

Mysteries Shrouded in Welcome

A coat that's lost, an old shoe found,
A cat that chats with the mailman bound.
The doorbell's chime has a silly tune,
It dances through halls, it croons like a loon.

A sun hat here, a glove over there,
Does someone live who's quite unaware?
They must have left a trail of cheer,
With every step, more laughter near!

Dust bunnies play hide and seek all day,
While lampshades speak of a silly ballet.
The keys by the window, who lost those gems?
Perhaps they were taken by playful friends!

In this place of stories and goofy glee,
Each corner holds some hilarity.
With every knock and giggle released,
The gathering spirits find love, at least!

The Untold Stories at the Edge

A sassy umbrella awaits the rain,
With polka dots sporting a silly chain.
The mat says welcome, but what does it mean?
To all the squirrels chasing a dream!

Gritty shoes kick up tales untold,
Of mischief and laughter that never grows old.
A broom in the corner, bristles askew,
Just giggles at parties hosted for two!

Faded sketches of scenes on the wall,
Where shadows once danced at a tiny ball.
What secrets lie in the floor's creak?
Whispers of socks taking a peak!

So take a step back, unwind your mind,
The stories are sprinkled, surprisingly kind.
Here joy bubbles up like a sweet fizzy drink,
We laugh with the air, no need to overthink!

Fading Footprints of Yesterday

Leaves scatter fast upon the ground,
In the corner, a mystery is found.
Footprints fading, they giggle and dance,
Were they left by a cat in a frenzied prance?

A squeaky toy in the hallway's embrace,
Echoes of laughter, what a wild chase!
A cap with a feather, a tale of its own,
Was it for a pirate who'd since overthrown?

The door guards secrets of shenanigans past,
Like a jester's gift that could never last.
Step into the world of peculiar plight,
Where every moment feels odd yet bright!

Peeking around, what wonders await,
A jigsaw of memories starting to mate.
In invisible ink, the laughter does stay,
In the joy of each moment, let's always play!

The Light Beneath the Archway

Under the arch, a glow now creeps,
Bringing chuckles, as nighttime peeps.
What secrets this arch has heard tonight,
From echoes of laughter, all pure delight!

The shadows shimmy like they know a dance,
While dust motes twirl, given a chance.
The laughter is loud, ridiculous and free,
As the critters join in a late-night spree!

Magical stories that bounce off the walls,
From a knock-knock joke to spontaneous calls.
The lampshades shimmer with collars of light,
Casting funny shapes in the soft, cozy night!

So gather your friends and don't miss the show,
The archway invites both the raucous and low.
In these moments where silliness shines,
The stories can stitch together our lines!

Hidden Voices of the Hallway

In the hallway, whispers creep,
Socks are running, oh so deep.
A cat's debate with a chair,
Who knew a lamp could wear a stare?

Noses sniffing at the snacks,
An echo of those clumsy acts.
From the corners, laughter's wail,
A dance-off with a broom's long tail.

Footsteps rumble, a race begins,
Dog sneezes, everyone grins.
A knock that's not a knock at all,
The doorbell's silent, can we call?

In this chaos, joy takes flight,
Mom's cooking something not quite right.
With secret giggles from the room,
The hallway's alive, dispelling gloom.

Stillness Beyond the Entrance

Beyond the threshold, silence reigns,
Dust bunnies dance in disdain.
A coat hangs low, its own surprise,
Echoed sighs from secret spies.

Potted plants forming a plot,
Wondering if they've been forgot.
The floor creaks, a tale to tell,
This quiet space knows all too well.

A shoe has wandered, all alone,
Lost in thoughts it's never known.
The welcome mat is overly bright,
Hoping for feet to join its sight.

Here the stillness sings its song,
In laughter echoed where we belong.
A superhero cape draped on a chair,
It's hard to be serious when fun's the air.

Home's First Breath

At dawn, the house lets out a yawn,
The toaster pops, a crisp new dawn.
Coffee brewing, what a scene,
Our hungry tummy, that's the queen!

The fridge hums tunes of playful cheer,
Where leftovers hide and dreams appear.
Curtains flutter, dancing light,
As morning spills in, oh what a sight!

The clock ticks loudly, it's out of fate,
Timing a show down at the gate.
Dishes argue in the sink,
Plates all huddle, thinking, "Think!"

Within these walls, joy keeps its sway,
In every corner, a game to play.
Oh, what a breath this place does share,
Where quirky stories hang in the air.

The First Embrace

As one steps in, warmth unfolds,
A hug of laughter, bright and bold.
The cushions plot a comfy scene,
Soft embraces, like a dream.

A jester's hat rests on a lamp,
Throw pillows boast their cushy camp.
This welcome mat, a feisty pal,
Inviting all for a merry gal.

Children squeal in each room's nook,
Imagination's wild storybook.
Towers of blocks, a creative spree,
Hugs from toys, oh they agree!

In every shadow, a giggle's found,
The heart of home makes a joyful sound.
From the first embrace, we can see,
This laughter space, it's all we need!

Unraveled by the Entrance

A shoe on the mat, what a sight,
A cat with a hat, oh what a fright!
Bags on the floor, snacks everywhere,
A dance-party vibe fills the air.

Laughter erupts, a tumble and roll,
Who needs a carpet when you've got soul?
The doorbell's ringing, a game on the go,
What's that behind it? A wild ballet show!

Socks on the cushions, cakes on the table,
A couch that's more wobbly than a fable!
The snacks keep disappearing, much to my glee,
As friends keep arriving, no time to be free!

Banners and streamers all twisted around,
Living room chaos in laughter is found.
Where's the punch? Who knows? We just cheer,
Unraveled delight, we're all gathered here!

The Unseen Welcome

You step in the room, what a curious sight,
The plants whisper secrets, they giggle in light.
There's cake in the air, and the carpet's a maze,
With socks as the bait for our funny game plays.

A shadow slips past, oh what could it be?
Is it a ghost, or just Fido with glee?
The welcome's enthusiastic, quirky, and wild,
Like a jester who's jiving, forever beguiled.

Pictures are leaning, they smile and they sway,
One frame with a wink—"You're in for a play!"
I trip over laughter, I tumble, I roll,
In this unseen welcome, I'm finding my soul.

Confetti and giggles dance in the breeze,
The welcome's contagious, an infectious tease.
So come one, come all, step in, feel the cheer,
The unseen is calling, funny friends gather near!

Where Shadows Linger

Each shadow a story, they wink as they pass,
Under the couch, there's a mystery… grass?
A giggle escapes, must be close at hand,
Where shadows linger, the jokes are well planned.

The lights flicker brightly, a disco of fate,
Dance with the silhouettes, they're never late.
A secret unfolds, as old tales unwind,
With shadows as friends, we leave worries behind.

The dust bunnies rise, they have much to share,
They tell us of journeys through wild stares.
With every soft laugh, the shadows expand,
In the warmth of the moments, together we stand.

So tiptoe on in, let your eyes adjust,
Embrace all the laughter, watch out for the dust!
For where shadows linger, good vibes always cling,
In the dance of the light, hear the joy that we bring.

Welcome to the Unknown

What's that at the door? A parade on the way!
With cupcakes on hats? Oh what a display!
The floor is alive, it shimmies and leaps,
As we make our grand entrance, our laughter just creeps.

Mysteries lurk in the cracks of the wall,
What's ticking over there? Just a clock taking a fall!
The snacks have their own bouncing around,
Welcome to the unknown, where joy can be found.

In corners, there's chit-chat and bubble-filled cheer,
Where friends weave their stories, and no one's austere.
So grab a loud drink, what's that flavor? Who knows!
It's fun in abundance wherever one goes!

With jokes in the air and a friendly surprise,
We'll stumble through chaos with glitter in our eyes.
So welcome aboard, to this wacky, wild ride,
In the land of the unknown, come take your stride!

Unveiling the Hallway

The hallway's a treasure, full of quaint little nooks,
Where dust bunnies gather like forgotten old books.
A shoe here, a coat there, a hat on a hook,
Each step brings a giggle, as the hallway just looks.

An echoing laugh from the room down the way,
Whispers of mischief at the end of the stay.
Puddles from boots seem to dance in their spray,
As we slide to the kitchen, for snacks on display.

Old photos are hanging, they grin with such zest,
A time-travel trip to the past, what a jest!
The cat's on a mission, but we must never rest,
For the hallway's our stage, and we are its guests.

With each twist and turn, a surprise in delight,
A stumble, a trip, shadows dance in the light.
The hallway's a circus, from day to the night,
We're laughing and running, what a comical sight!

First Step Stories

Every creak in the floor tells a tale of the day,
In a world so peculiar, where socks go astray.
First steps full of laughter, a skip and a sway,
Each misstep a memory, oh what a bouquet!

Slippers, not shoes, had a party unplanned,
Wobbling around like a band in a stand.
Chasing a pet, who just doesn't understand,
The joy in the journey, oh isn't it grand!

From spider's brave web, a dance in the air,
To ghosts of the past with a playful flair.
Each first step is magic, a whimsical dare,
As we stumble through stories, we find everywhere.

So here's to the laughter each footfall will bring,
Where the journey begins and the memories sing.
For every first step in the hallway a fling,
Turns everyday moments into a joyful string!

Beneath the Doormat

Beneath where we wipe off our shoes every day,
Lies a world full of secrets that dance and that play.
Mice throw a party, keeping boredom at bay,
While dust bunnies gossip, "Where did Fred stray?"

Forgotten old shopping lists, tangled and worn,
Whisper loud stories since the day they were torn.
Each letter a memory, like seeds they are sown,
As beneath the doormat, a giggle's been born.

An occasional shoe from a traveler's quest,
Makes friends with the spatula, isn't that best?
The crumbs with a promise of snacks, they invest,
In a tiny adventure, come join this wild fest!

So remember each time that you reach for the latch,
Underneath lives a tale in a whimsical patch.
For laughter and joy are found not in a catch,
But under the mat where the jests always hatch!

Sanctuary of Silent Steps

In corridors narrow, we tiptoe with grace,
Navigating shadows in a hilarious chase.
Each silent step giggles, it's a comical race,
In this sacred space where we find our own place.

The creaking old floorboards like secrets they keep,
Echoing softly, urging silence, not sleep.
A laugh from the restroom, oh, the secret's too deep,
In this sanctuary, memories jump in a heap.

A vibrant collection of shoes left around,
In this haven of chaos, citadel profound.
Finding doodles on walls where art is unbound,
We discover such joy in what's here to be found.

So embrace every moment, the whispers, the fun,
In this journey of silliness, we all come undone.
For each silent step opens a door to the sun,
In a sanctuary where laughter has just begun!

Gathering Place of Souls

In the hall where laughter rings,
We gather 'round like crazy springs.
Jokes fly high, and snacks abound,
A circus here, where joy is found.

Old photos grin from dusty frames,
Each face a twist of love and games.
The cat's our jester, stealing treats,
While we swap tales of our wild feats.

Fur coats flutter, and shoes collide,
A dance floor grows where pets abide.
To trip and giggle is the goal,
At this madcap gathering of souls.

When sunset hits, the shadows sprawl,
We'll toast to life, and catch a fall.
No ones left behind, all here to stay,
In this nutty haven, come what may.

The Unsaid Greeting

A nod exchanged, a coffee spill,
With quirky smiles that fit the bill.
We share a space, the silence loud,
At times, it feels like we're a crowd.

The welcome mat is rather frayed,
Yet here we jump, unafraid.
A wink that says, 'I see you there,'
Though none of us would truly dare.

Chairs wobble under chief repair,
As tales unfold, we're nearly bare.
The fridge hums softly in the back,
While words of wisdom start to crack.

We pass the snacks like secret notes,
In this dim light where laughter floats.
No need for spoken words or spins,
In silence, oh, our friendship wins.

Secrets Behind Closed Doors

Whispers gather like little sprites,
Behind the wood, as day turns nights.
Children's giggles, muffled, tight,
Hold onto dreams, out of sight.

The garden blooms with tales unspun,
Of where the lost socks hide, just fun.
Tales of mischief, sock-stealing gnomes,
Where all are kings inside their homes.

The walls lean in, to catch a grin,
A trade of puns – let laughs begin.
With every schmooze, the air grows warm,
Late-night secrets form a charm.

Behind those panels, tales unique,
With shades of laughter, gentle sneak.
Unveiling hearts, each twist a win,
In secret spaces, friendships spin.

Once a Threshold

Once a threshold, a step to roam,
Ring the bell – welcome home!
The floorboards creak with every guest,
Like old friends sharing their best.

The luggage piled in a haphazard heap,
With snacks and stories, oh, so deep.
Fingers point at silly hats,
As laughter soars like friendly chats.

In corners lurk old dusty books,
And curious glances, sly little looks.
We dip our toes in a pool of fun,
As friendships meld 'til day is done.

With every knock, a smile anew,
The door swings wide; we break right through.
A world awaiting, beyond the frame,
In this crazy place where none are tame.

Guardians of the Entrance

Two little gnomes guard the way,
With pointy hats and smiles that play.
They wave their arms, loud and clear,
"No shoes allowed, leave them right here!"

A cat sits proud upon the mat,
Staring down the mailman, fat.
With a flick of tail, she claims her throne,
"You knock, you wait, this is my zone!"

The doorbell sings a silly tune,
Bouncing echoes, a comedic swoon.
As friends trip in with snacks galore,
"Welcome! But crumbs—leave at the door!"

And if you think you'll slip on through,
The giant boots will greet you too.
They trip and tumble all around,
Guardians of giggles, with laughter found.

Threshold of Dreams

Step upon this doormat bright,
Where socks and slippers unite in flight.
A world awaits, just beyond the frame,
Where laundry piles morph into fame.

The dust bunnies wear tiny crowns,
As they rule the kingdom of pants and gowns.
They dance a jig with the forgotten sock,
At this threshold, time ticks like a clock.

The echoes of giggles float like a breeze,
As family tales bring you to your knees.
The mysteries hidden in every nook,
Are waiting for you, so come take a look!

With a wink from the latch and creak of the floor,
Step lightly, dear friend; it's never a bore.
For in this place where nonsense gleams,
You're welcomed forever, in wild dreams.

The Quiet Welcome

Come as you are, the sign's all clear,
A welcome with coffee, and maybe a beer.
The cushion's plush, the cat's quite sweet,
While the fridge hums softly, oh, what a treat!

Pajamas are the dress code, so chic,
Forget about heels, it's comfort we seek.
In this haven, every toss and turn,
Brings laughter and stories; for that we yearn.

So kick off your shoes, let worries be gone,
The doormat's a dance floor—come twirl till dawn!
A smirk on the walls, a chuckle so bold,
In this quiet place, isn't life pure gold?

The echoed whispers of friends' delight,
Transform a plain evening into pure light.
With every giggle that fills the air,
You'll know you're home, nowhere else compares.

A Haven's Embrace

In this tiny nook, enchantment's at play,
With memories blooming like flowers in May.
The door swings open, a chorus begins,
With squeaks and squeals that tickle your skins.

A doormat of mischief and graceful flair,
Welcomes your laughter, it's always aware.
The laundry pile winks, a never-end joke,
"Care to join me? I'm comfy," it spoke!

The mirror reflects your funniest face,
As you strut through the threshold, entering grace.
With cushions like clouds, and cushions like fun,
Each visit a saga, where all can just run.

So grab a snack, let the silliness flow,
For in this warm haven, you always can glow.
The doorway's a portal, where joy intertwines,
In this sweet embrace, the heart always shines.

Beyond the Latch

A cat sat posing, proud and grand,
With a sprinkle of dust on a tiny band.
He guards the secrets of the old shoe rack,
While dreaming of mice, in a world so slack.

The fridge hums softly, a melody sweet,
Pasta and pickles in a rhythmic beat.
The toaster pops bread like a jolly laugh,
As spills and crumbs dance in their own gaff.

Beneath the coat hooks, a hat takes flight,
With a jaunty tilt, oh what a sight!
The coat's gripping tightly to the cold's embrace,
It's a comedy show in this cozy space.

Footsteps stumble as they hit the mat,
Who would have thought it could be like that?
A dance of silliness at the day's end,
Where laughter and chaos always blend.

The Heart's Vestibule

A jiggly jelly sits on the shelf,
Wobbling blandly, all by itself.
Do you dare slice it, with glee or fright?
It shudders and quivers, oh what a sight!

Socks pair up like old friends, quite neat,
Yet one always goes missing, a sneaky feat.
Like a game of hide and seek they play,
Where's the other sock? It'd run away!

The hallway echoes with comical squeaks,
From shoes left behind or playful peeks.
Each step is a giggle, a misstep too,
In this wacky realm, where chaos ensues.

An old mirror reflects a ghostly grin,
Making poses as light spills in.
A funny little moment caught in the glass,
Where laughter lives on, as the hours pass.

Echoes of Warmth

With a creak, the door swings with flair,
A welcoming gust tosses back my hair.
A chair lets out a sigh, a peaceful tone,
As dust motes dance in their little zone.

The kettle whistles like a merry bird,
Promises of tea, so sweetly stirred.
But first, that spoon goes sailing away,
Into the wild, where the lost cutlery play!

Old coats whisper secrets of past shoeprints,
They chat about journeys, and wayward hints.
A scarf giggles softly, draped on a hook,
While dusty shelves hide tales from a book.

Each echo carries warmth, oh what a thrill,
In the rhythmic hums of the evening chill.
Bathed in laughter and playful delight,
This antics-filled place shines ever so bright.

Silhouettes at Dusk

The shadows stretch long, like a lazy cat,
Lurking by corners, where we once sat.
They dance and they weave in the fading light,
A parody show of the day turning night.

Jackets hang awkwardly, arms akimbo,
They sway with the laughter of an unseen limbo.
Chairs wobble in mischief, a comedy scene,
As a wiggle and giggle spill in between.

The clock ticks a tune, but the rhythm's offbeat,
Is it time for dinner or time for a treat?
The hallway chuckles at the day's final jest,
In a house full of whims, we are truly blessed.

As evening paints patterns in shades of gray,
The mischief resumes in a lovable way.
Together we stand, in this quirky nook,
Creating our own tales, in laughter, we cook.

Beyond the Portal

A cat patrols, a guard so proud,
With whiskers twitching, he meows loud.
The welcome mat, a stage of play,
Where shoes are toys that dance away.

A sock on the floor, what mischief's there?
The door swings wide, as chaos gets rare.
Neighbors peek, with curious glee,
At antics that tumble, oh what a spree!

A broom becomes a knight's fair steed,
In this kingdom of shoes, cats, and weeds.
Laughter echoes in every nook,
As the door tells tales in every look.

So step on through, into the fun,
Where giggles and grumbles harmonize as one.
With every creak and squeak, we find,
Life's little quirks, so sweetly designed.

Flickers of Hearth Light

There's a light that flickers, not quite bright,
Bestowing shadows that dance in the night.
The fridge hums softly, a gentle croon,
Whispers of snacks, like a funky tune.

A misplaced shoe, a left behind hat,
Socks on the lamp, imagine that!
Each corner holds secrets, some pert, some sly,
As we trip over giggles and a quick goodbye.

Popcorn goals or a wild, wild chase,
As laughter fills up this welcoming space.
With every breeze, the curtains sway,
Inviting us to join in the play.

So gather 'round, forget the grind,
In the warmth of the glow, humor we find.
Let the flickers guide you to joy's embrace,
In this haven where smiles find their place.

The Doorway's Tongue

What secrets lie in the opening wide?
A dog with a stick, he's filled with pride.
A mischievous grin, the doorway winks,
Spinning tales with every creak that clinks.

One foot in and one foot out,
A race with a squirrel, who's winning? No doubt!
A hat on a hook, a ghost of a friend,
As the doorway giggles, will the fun never end?

Bubbles and trinkets, treasures abound,
In the hallway, strange echoes resound.
With a wink and a nudge, it's always a jest,
Entering life's stage, we're truly blessed.

So when you approach this whimsical veil,
Remember the smiles, the laughter, the tale.
Each entry's a promise of moments to share,
As the doorway's tongue twirls, full of flair.

Memories in the Foyer

In the foyer, laughter holds a seat,
As dust bunnies dance on little feet.
With coats like capes, we swirl and twirl,
Magic is found in this little swirl.

A meow and a bark, a playdate surprise,
As slippers become rockets that fly through the skies.
Puddles of giggles form beneath the mat,
As the door creeks open, inviting the chat.

A wobbly table and a teetering chair,
Guide our adventures to everywhere.
Each moment a gem, in the hallway's glow,
With echoes of fun, we play, and we grow.

So let's hold these memories, quick as a breeze,
In the foyer, we find joy with such ease.
With a tickle of laughter, we wrap up the day,
For this goofy beginning is here to stay.

Uncharted Spaces

Boxes stacked in wild display,
Mismatched shoes, a game to play.
The dog claims a chair, thinks he's the king,
In this odd world, laughter takes wing.

Sticky notes cover every spot,
A calendar filled with plans forgot.
A treasure hunt in my own abode,
Finding socks when the laundry's exploded.

Jars of cookies, half full and old,
Mysteries waiting, stories untold.
The cat patrols, a stalker so sly,
In this uncharted space, we laugh and cry.

With each step taken, the laughter grows,
In this bizarre maze, anything goes.
Join me in this whimsical chase,
For life's a comedy in this cluttered place.

Veil of the Hall

Creaking floors sing a funny tune,
Dancing shadows by the light of the moon.
A picture's askew, a smile wide,
Capturing memories that can't hide.

The coat rack stands like a quirky friend,
Hats and scarves that twist and bend.
Each guest that enters sparks a new tale,
Of mishaps and joys with laughter to hail.

The hallway's a runway, a space to strut,
We make silly faces, embrace the nut.
A burst of giggles, a tumble, a fall,
In the veil of the hall, we're a circus, after all.

With stories spilling from every crack,
Echoes of laughter urging us back.
In this curtain of laughter, we take our stance,
For life's a grand show, let's join in the dance!

Between the Walls

Whispers hide where shadows linger,
Old secrets tickle each curious finger.
The walls waddle with tales to tell,
In silly voices, we weave our spell.

Dust bunnies hold a grand debate,
Competing for space, oh, isn't it great?
A sock on the floor, a prize on the quest,
In this funny chaos, we're truly blessed.

Each nook and cranny, a mystery grand,
With memories waiting, hand in hand.
An echo of laughter drifts through the halls,
Between the walls, the joy never stalls.

So let's raise the roof with our silly song,
For life's a romp where we all belong.
Between these walls, in this jubilant throng,
We gather in laughter, forever strong.

A Step Into Solitude

A door creaks open with a hint of glee,
In solitude's arms, I find my spree.
A comfy chair calls with echoes of cheer,
In this cozy retreat, I've not a fear.

The world outside seems a circus absurd,
But I've got tea, stories shall be stirred.
The cat gives a nod, we make a fine pair,
In moments of quiet, life feels rare.

A sock puppet show with no audience near,
Each joke told alone brings giggles to cheer.
Outside may be wild, a hurricane's race,
But here in my bubble, I've all the space.

A step into solitude, a dance with my mind,
Where silliness flows, and peace I find.
In my happy realm, oh, what fun I see,
Laughter's the language, just my cat and me.

Opening to New Thoughts

A knock was heard, quite unexpected,
I peeped out what I first suspected.
A cat with socks, a squirrel in gear,
What a strange parade, oh dear oh dear!

With each new face, my mind did twirl,
Thoughts unraveled like a spun-up pearl.
They shared their tales of wacky glee,
A dance-off started, just wait and see!

Behold the antics, crazy and wild,
I laughed so hard, I felt like a child.
A world of antics right at my feet,
A silly chapter that couldn't be beat!

So here's the lesson, I've learned today,
Open you door and let laughter play.
For once you peek, oh what a sight,
New thoughts swirl in, dancing with light!

The Edges of Comfort

The door stood wide with a creak and a squeak,
A place where chaos and comfort peek.
I ventured forth, my heart all aflutter,
A funny feeling, like stepping in butter!

In walked a llama in shades, oh my!
"Do you live here?" I couldn't help but cry.
With a wink and a nod, he danced in place,
I chuckled so hard, I lost my grace!

Then came a frog with a top hat on,
Singing a jingle to cheer everyone.
The room filled with laughter, joy in the air,
As unicorns pranced with nary a care!

In this odd mix of comfort and fun,
I found new edges, shining like the sun.
So when in doubt, just open and see,
What wacky adventures come knocking for free!

Shadows at the Opening

Shadows danced near the glimmering light,
Curious figures with laughs oh so bright.
A bear with a bowler sauntered by fast,
Chasing a shadow—what a curious cast!

Then came a hedgehog, all spindly and quick,
He tripped on a shoelace, it was quite the trick!
"Didn't see that coming," I laughed from my perch,
As he gave a bow, admitting his search.

The door still swung, inviting delight,
More silly shadows danced into sight.
With giggles and jabs, the room filled with cheer,
I ended up rolling—oh, what a queer!

So next time you fear the shadows outside,
Just open the door and let laughter glide.
For once you do, the shadows come play,
Funny little friends who brighten your day!

A Canvas of Welcome

A door that swings wide with colors galore,
Each shade of laughter inviting much more.
A canvas alive with winks and with grins,
Every splash tells tales, where the fun begins!

I welcomed a penguin with rollerblades on,
He zoomed through my hall, like a well-crafted con.
Then came a gnome with a marshmallow hat,
His jokes flew like confetti, oh what of that!

A ladybug joined with a giggle and spin,
She said, "Why not dance? Let the fun begin!"
We twirled and we whirled, oh, what a view,
A carnival sprung from the colors so true!

So paint your door with moments of cheer,
A gallery bright to welcome all near.
For every new visitor, a stroke in the scheme,
A canvas of welcome, a whimsical dream!

Secrets in the Vestibule

Behind the shoes, a treasure lies,
Mismatched socks, a grand surprise!
Coats hang like ghosts with stories to tell,
Lost umbrellas bid farewell.

Laundry baskets overflow with fate,
Stains and crumbs that just can't wait.
A hat with a feather, who knew it could be?
The closet's a time warp, just wait and see!

Dirt tracked in like a racetrack's art,
The welcome mat is losing its heart.
Key hooks that laugh at the keys they lack,
It's a circus of chaos, but who needs a snack?

A mirror reflects the faces we've worn,
In this tiny space, so many adorned.
Yet silliness reigns, with joyful, sly wit,
In these silly secrets, we always fit!

Whispers of Recent Guests

A knock at the door, then laughter arises,
Footprints of friends in whimsical sizes.
Leftover snacks in a half-open bag,
Who knew a party could feel like a drag?

Jokes traded like currency, echoes in the hall,
A flick of the light, someone just took a fall!
This cozy nook, a gathering space,
With tales and confessions that quicken the pace.

There's glitter from crafts that flew through the air,
And a wig that was worn just to give folks a scare.
Forgotten drinks perched on the ledge,
As laughter still lingers, a jovial pledge.

The fireplace whispers warm, silly thoughts,
As memories of shenanigans make happy knots.
In this quaint little space, we cherish delight,
For friendships are treasures that shine ever bright!

Unlocked Memories

A rickety shelf with a vase that's chipped,
Where memories linger, some slightly flipped.
Dust bunnies dance in the timid light,
Each trinket uncovers a whimsical sight.

Toys from long ages, still lodged in a box,
A jester's hat, and mismatched socks.
Grandma's old cane with a story to weave,
Oh, what treasures the past can leave!

Photographs strewn like confetti in air,
Each snapshot a giggle, each glance a dare.
Granny with cake on her chocolatey nose,
Every 'remember when' brings a burst of prose.

Each unlocked door whispers secrets held tight,
In memories' arena, all is delight.
From silly to serious, this tapestry's spun,
In this vibrant mess, life's far from done!

The Hidden Nook

A cluttered corner with cushions askew,
This nook is our haven, where giggles imbue.
Piles of old blankets and tales of the old,
With antics of cats, both brazen and bold.

Crumbs from the snacks that we snuck in to munch,
Hiding from chores with our crafty little hunch.
Retro games stacked as high as the skies,
We get lost in laughter, much to our surprise.

Glimmers of sunlight in funky designs,
Here, we create and cross silly lines.
The radio crackles with tunes from the past,
We dance like no one's watching, our shadows are cast.

In our cozy nook, the world fades away,
Just laughter and whimsy in a playful ballet.
So here's to the corners of joy that we find,
In the hidden nooks, we're forever entwined!

Veiled Moments After Daylight

The cat's on the mat, with a look so sly,
I tiptoe in quietly, trying not to cry.
A pile of shoes, they tumble and roll,
As I dodge the lost toys that squarely patrol.

With snacks in hand, I inch to the fridge,
But the dog's got a plan, a foolproof bridge.
He leaps with a woof, my treats all fly,
In this chaos, I'm left to wonder why.

The kids burst in laughing, they've found my stash,
While I search for a way to reclaim some cash.
Dress-up hats fly; they're quite the delight,
Only to end with me losing the fight.

So here's to the moments, both silly and bright,
Where laughter and chaos weave day into night.
In the corners of life, joy often prevails,
As we trip over laughter, on these wondrous trails.

Footprints in the Entryway

A trail of tiny shoes, all over the floor,
Each print tells a story, it's hard to ignore.
Rio the puppy, with mud on his paws,
Just waltzed through my hallway without any cause.

I shuffle and shuffle, trying to clean,
Only to find more surprises unseen.
The kids' sticky fingers, they reached for the snacks,
Their giggling laughter still echoes in packs.

As I scrub and I wipe, there's a sock on the wall,
Was it meant for the wash, or to add to the brawl?
With every new footprint, my sanity fades,
Yet in this wild mess, great joy cascades.

Oh, footprints of play, you weave such a tale,
In the madness of home, I'll gladly set sail.
Here's to the trails, both unwelcome and true,
For every wild story, there's laughter in view.

A Doorway to Reflection

A mirror hangs crooked, it's seen better days,
I stand here just pondering life's quirky ways.
With a smudge on my cheek and a roll of my eyes,
My reflection might chuckle, or maybe just sighs.

Next to the coat rack, it's holding the dreams,
Of hats that have vanished, or slipped through the seams.
A drawer full of memories, odd keys and more,
Each trinket a whisper from moments before.

Jackets of laughter still hang on the line,
Like ghosts of good times, they shimmer and shine.
In the chaos of life, I find little gems,
In the hustle and bustle, I cherish my friends.

So here in this space, I embrace all the quirks,
In the doorway of laughter where humor still lurks.
Life's little surprises come wrapped in delight,
As I pause for a moment, and bask in the light.

Embraced by Walls

These walls hold the echoes of family cheers,
As we trip over laughter and stumbles, my dears.
With crayons on paper, the art's quite a sight,
Though it looks like a baboon designed it outright.

The laundry pile's growing, I lost track of time,
While the kids commandeer my once tidy clime.
Toys litter the floor like an obstacle course,
It's a wild, wacky ride, with no sign of remorse.

As I cling to my coffee, the dog's got a sock,
He prances around, thinking he'll be the rock.
Each day's a new chapter, a thrilling delight,
Embraced by these walls, we dance through the night.

So here's to the chaos, the love that we share,
In the humdrum of life, we find joy everywhere.
Laughter, my dear friends, is the key to it all,
In this cozy nook, we forever stand tall.

The Hidden Invitation

A sock on the floor, what a sight!
It waves like a flag, in the morning light.
Inviting me in for a game of hide and seek,
Who knew my home was so full of cheek?

A cat in the cupboard, and a dog on a chair,
Both looking guilty with their cute little stare.
They've thrown a wild party while I was away,
Now they prance around, like they own the day.

The fridge is a treasure, crammed full and bright,
Leftovers whisper, "Come feast, it's a delight!"
A half-eaten cake calls, with frosting all gone,
Do I share with the pets, or eat it alone?

So here's to the secrets that dwell in my space,
A fortress of laughter, my own happy place.
With funny surprises around every bend,
Who knew home sweet home could be such a trend?

Passage to the Heart

A narrow hallway with echoes of cheer,
The voices of loved ones always near.
Pictures go gossiping tucked on the wall,
They've seen all my stumbles, my rise and fall.

A misplaced shoe tells a tale of its own,
How I darted out late, nearly overthrown.
The clock keeps on laughing, time slipping away,
While I juggle my chaos, in this grand ballet.

Spilled cereal crunches, a crunchy delight,
A sprinkle of laughter at breakfast, just right.
The coffee pot whistles, "Where's my next fill?"
As friends share their stories; I've got time to kill.

Through this comedic space with its twists and turns,
I guide my way onward, with love always burns.
A passage of giggles, a hallway of smiles,
Life's a funny journey, let's enjoy the miles!

Quiet Corners of Home

In the quietest corner, the cat takes a nap,
Dreaming of fish, in her fantasy trap.
A pillow's the throne for her royal decree,
"Gentle servants, bring snacks, and let me be free!"

Under the table, a stash of old toys,
Dust bunnies frolic with the lost little joys.
The vacuum strikes fear, like a monster so bold,
Hiding those treasures, once shiny, now old.

Stepping on Legos, a homecoming feat,
My toes dance like crazy, it's not bittersweet.
A laugh in the hallway, it echoes, it flows,
These quiet corners are where humor grows.

So here in these nooks, so cozy, so still,
Lies laughter unspoken, and heart-filled thrills.
In our little corners, where oddities roam,
We find all the giggles that turn into home.

A Glimpse Through the Keyhole

Peeking through the keyhole, oh what a view,
A dancer in socks, with an old broom to woo.
She spins and she twirls, her audience laughs,
While the plants in their pots join the crazy giraffes.

In the kitchen is chaos, pots clank and clang,
Chasing that lid, oh, it's quite the yang.
A dog in the oven? No, that's just wrong,
But to him, it's a kingdom, where he can't go wrong.

The oven door creaks, whispering tales,
Of cookies that burned and the smell of old fails.
But laughter is worth it, for each little 'oops,'
When we cook up our dreams, and mix in the goofs.

So spy with delight through this keyhole of glee,
Where life's little moments are meant to be free.
For each funny mishap is a reason to cheer,
In the magical world of our cozy frontier.

www.ingramcontent.com/pod-product-compliance
Lightning Source LLC
Chambersburg PA
CBHW070314120526
44590CB00017B/2670